LEADERSHIP
A Matter of Faith

D1062944

LEADERSHIP
A Matter of Faith

5 Essential Guideposts to
Steer Your Career & Life to Create
a Lasting Legacy

RICH MILLER

To all leaders of today, we need you

TABLE OF CONTENTS

PROLOGUE

My palms are sweaty and my throat feels dry. I'm surprised by this. As a CEO for more than twenty years, I have vast public speaking experience. I frequently address groups of all sizes, and even television cameras don't faze me. But as I wait to step into the auditorium to deliver the commencement address to a packed Knott Arena at Mount St. Mary's University, I am nervous as a cat!

The date is Sunday, May 14, 2017. Mother's Day. Two weeks earlier, I had received a call from the university president asking me if I could give the speech at the graduation ceremony as their scheduled speaker had to cancel. The invitation was a great honor indeed, but we already had plans with our children and grandchildren for that day. My wife of four decades looked at me and simply said, "You're going to do this. It's a once-in-a-lifetime opportunity."

Mary Lee was right.

Now as I proceed into the arena with the university trustees, faculty and students, I realize what I'm feeling isn't nerves exactly, but good old fashioned emotion, plain and simple. I feel gratitude, deep glorious gratitude, in every part of my being. This speech means more to me than just words of wisdom and encouragement to a group of young people. As I step before the podium, it's like my life had come full circle.

I had been asked to become a Trustee of the university in January 2017, which was a tremendous honor for me as this school has a special place in my heart for a number of reasons. I had loved my four years at Mount St. Mary's, entering as an undergrad in 1970. I met some good friends and built wonderful relationships during those years, many of which are still present in my life today. I proposed to the love of my life, Mary Lee, in 1975 in the Grotto of Lourdes on this beautiful campus. And it was at the end of my time at Mount St. Mary's that my faith and true relationship with God took root.

The spring of my senior year was a terribly difficult period of my life. A tragic accident left me unable to attend my own college commencement ceremony in 1974, and my parents had to accept my diploma for me. And now here I was, at graduation at my alma mater. As we begin the procession into the arena, I strongly feel the presence of God. *Congratulations, Rich! You made it! I love you!*

I have made it. I'm blessed indeed. My family is my joy and I've had an extremely successful career. The kid from South Philly grew up and learned how to be a leader. And helping others grow in their leadership capacity has become my new mission.

The lessons gleaned in my life were shared with the audience that day, to a standing ovation. The knowledge I have garnered is what I feel compelled to write for you here. The following chapters will give you a crash course into what I consider true leadership.

Let me tell you up front, there is no magic bullet. If you are searching for a quick fix or a Band-aid or a magic wand, keep looking. If you are a leader at the helm of your company, but only focused on short term profits, this book is not for you. But if you are in for the long term game, let me provide you a proven philosophy along with concrete tactics, my "guideposts," that can shepherd you. What I lay out can help you in your current position, and you can take the knowledge and roadmap with you even if/when you change companies. This strategy here is for your whole life.

Over the span of my four-decades long career, I have met many talented leaders—extraordinary people—but some have lost their way or perhaps don't fully know their role. Being a CEO and a leader is a complex task, but we can keep our priorities and strategy simple.

When you have clear steps to take, you create a solid path for yourself, and one that others can follow.

My core philosophy is that we are all lifelong learners (or we all can be, if we choose) and leadership is among those things we can learn. Yes, it's true that many of our ideas and beliefs are formed when we are young, by our parents, our environment, and society, and sometimes those beliefs are pretty rigid, and often we hang on to them too tightly. For me going away to college allowed me to grow as a person. I was exposed to all kinds of new ideas and a spigot opened. I gathered insights from a wide variety of people. Learning to accept different people and different ideas was a breakthrough. Becoming an open thinker can happen at any age. That is my advice to you as you delve into these pages and as you move forward in your life. Be open. Don't pre-judge people and don't pre-judge the simplicity of this book.

If you are ready to discover how to establish a career, and a life, that you will be able to look back on with pride and gratitude, let's begin. I hope you enjoy and I thank you for reading.

Rich Miller, May 14, 2020

MY STORY
PLEASE DON'T LET ME DIE

Back in the 1950s and 60s, most of the neighborhoods in South Philadelphia were known by what Catholic parish you belonged to. I grew up near King of Peace parish at 26th and Reed Streets. My parents, Joseph and Mary, were factory workers at Baker Clothing located on the corner of those same two streets.

My mother was Italian Catholic, and my father was Jewish. This made our family unique in South Philly, and as a kid on the playground, unique was not what you wanted to be. Even though my father converted to Catholicism prior to their marriage in 1950, we were still considered different. Growing up was not always easy at times given my ethnicity. I felt a backlash, silent and said out loud. Kids in the neighborhood would sling racial slurs at my older brother and me, the most mild of which was "half breed." There were times we were shunned from playing sports and games because of our so-called mixed identity, but I never shied away from my culture. I was proud of it.

My dad's family was not happy, to say the least, when he converted. In fact, the only person on my dad's side of the family who attended my parents' Catholic church wedding was his brother, Bernie. As the years went on, however, my dad's family grew closer to us and I cherish my memories of taking the bus and train to northeast Philly (Little Tel-Aviv) to visit my Jewish grandparents. My Grandmom Miller was a terrific cook—her apple cake and sour cream cake were to die for. She was a modern woman yet still steeped in many of the old traditions. My grandmom had lost relatives in the Holocaust and her broad wisdom left an indelible imprint on me.

My Jewish/Italian background had a major impact on my thinking today. One faith was not right or better. We honored both traditions. Taking part in the Seder meal was not just about the food, the learnings were phenomenal. Both traditions were similar but different. I remember commemorating Passover on a Wednesday with the Jewish side of the family and celebrating Easter the following Sunday at Aunt Mary's in our Little Italy neighborhood. My life was rich with outstanding heritage, cultures and food. I've often joked about the fact of having so much heartburn and guilt growing up given my background of both Italian and Jewish.

I didn't realize it as a kid, of course, but being exposed to differing faiths shaped my ability to understand, evaluate, and accept differing opinions. In the workplace, the entire staff and the executive team all come from varied points of view. To be able to process and balance divergent perspectives without judgement is a worthy characteristic for a CEO.

The formative years are just that, they form us. Our upbringing shapes us to some degree and most of our ideas and beliefs when we are young come from our parents and family. When it was time to go to college, I chose a small Catholic school in rural Maryland, Mount Saint Mary's. My parents did what they could to help with the expenses, but college was a heavy financial burden for working class parents. Most of the student body back then at the Mount were from middle class families like mine so borrowing money for tuition and taking on a part-time job were not out of the ordinary.

I worked weekends as a waiter at the Sheraton Hotel in Gettysburg, PA, right over the Maryland state line. The tips were good at the upscale restaurant and I enjoyed the camaraderie with my co-workers. One Spring Friday night in 1974, my senior year, my drive back to campus after work changed the trajectory of my life.

The night was crisp and cool as I got into my '62 Volkswagen bug. The trip started off like all the other late Friday night commutes after my shift ended. It was midnight, I was tired, but I was happy for the cash. This night I was thinking about my upcoming finals.

I don't remember anything after that.

I woke up with a concrete bridge abutment in my face. I had fallen asleep at the wheel and hit the abutment going 40 miles per hour. My left leg got caught under the seat as I was thrown from the car, snapping the tibia and fibula bones in my left leg. The car rolled over and landed on top of me. I was trapped underneath. The smell of gasoline was all around. *Is the car going to explode? Am I going to die?*

Gasping for air with my one good lung, (I didn't know it then—I didn't know the extent of any of my injuries then—my left lung had collapsed), I begged God to save me. *Please don't let me die! Please! I don't want to die like this! Please, God, help me! I don't want to die!*

In and out consciousness, I laid there for three hours until a trucker found me. Air lifted to the University of Maryland-Baltimore's shock trauma unit, I was placed on a ventilator and required dialysis due to total renal failure. Packed in ice to control my body temperature, fighting for my life, I thought I was not going to pull through. My chances for survival were not good. Doctors told my parents that they estimated a 10% chance of me making it.

But obviously, I did survive.

I did not die that night nor in the long days ahead. My time in the hospital seemed without end. Instead of being overjoyed to be alive, I was a very sick and angry twenty-one-year-old young man. Those weeks of recovery were filled with some positive moments certainly, but also many dark ones. Being on dialysis and a ventilator is not what a college senior plans on in the weeks before graduation. As much as I hated being on the ventilator, being weaned was terrifying. Whenever I was being weaned it felt like I was drowning. It was then I realized that breathing is a learned activity. Never again did I take ordinary inhaling and exhaling for granted.

For the highs and successes, there were prevalent lows. The Shock Trauma unit was a closed unit, all drab green walls, no windows and the entire staff dressed in that same drab green color scrubs. Visitors were not allowed regularly. There was no real contact with the outside world. Taking Percocet for the pain, I felt trapped in my body and in my circumstance. The lack of light in my external surroundings mirrored the lack of light I felt internally, and I was slipping into depression.

One nurse saw what was happening to me. Nurse Joanne took a personal interest in her patients and it became her mission to keep me alert and engaged with life. If not for her, I am not sure what would have happened with my mental state. Joanne found out that I was a devoted Philadelphia Flyers hockey fan, and the Flyers were making a run for their first Stanley Cup. She brought the Philadelphia Inquirer newspaper to my room and read me the accounts of the games, and all the results from the sports pages. Remember, this was 1974. There was no internet. Joanne made a point to secure the physical newspaper and read to me every day. Never underestimate the power of a small kindness. Joanne kept a real lifeline alive for me, one that had nothing to do with medical technology. She found one thread of hope that would keep me going and she didn't let go of it.

At night when I couldn't sleep, Joanne put me in a wheelchair and wheeled me down by the nurses' station so I could be around people and activity and conversation. Nurse Joanne gave me human connection. She was the kind of nurse and caregiver that saw her patients as human beings. Joanne realized that the scars on the body were not the only scars from serious trauma. She treated me like a whole person. The doctors and entire nursing team took care of my physical trauma, but I owe my mental rehabilitation to Joanne. I am forever grateful to her, and all these years later, I can still hear her voice as she read to me the newspaper articles about my beloved hockey team.

My recovery progressed, but the constant suctioning of my lungs plus the tremendous fatigue from being on dialysis took its toll on me emotionally. It also looked like my leg was going to have to be amputated. I was starting to hit rock bottom again.

But then… one night lying in bed wide awake, yet another sleepless night, a great light and a strong presence filled my hospital room. There was such an energy and goodness, a palpable spirit. I felt my soul and body being energized, fortified and lifted. In that instant I knew God was there and with me. This moment was unlike anything I had ever experienced. Not through spoken word but via my soul, He told me that I would be going home soon. Very clearly I understood, *You're going to be okay, Rich.*

In church and growing up in my faith, I had sensed what I would call the presence of God before, but nothing like this.

I buzzed for the nurse.

"Get my parents on the phone! I have to talk to them now. I have incredible news!"

Within ten days, I was headed home, with my leg. They didn't have to amputate. Upon discharge, every doctor and nurse in the unit came to say goodbye with tears in their eyes. My dad later told me that one of the physicians said my survival was a miracle.

All I know was that my life was changed forever.

I didn't heal spontaneously or immediately. My left leg was in a full cast and if you've ever had a cast, you know it itches! Whatever object I stuck down in there to scratch my knee also made a cut and an infection ensued. The pain was horrendous. After the cast was removed, the leg still had severe nerve damage and I required a brace. I had to teach myself to walk again. And I had to teach myself to live without Percocet. I had become addicted. I was readmitted back the hospital for withdrawal from the Percocet and the pain of withdrawal was excruciating. Then recovery really kicked in. And I made my way back into the land of the living.

That's my story. What I know now from this vantage point in life is that everyone has a story. We all have had our life-changing moments. Some are burning bushes. Some are more subtle. This accident and my time in the hospital was my kicking-off into adulthood, and the episode that set me on the path for what would become my life's work.

During all those weeks in the hospital, I saw the positives and negatives of healthcare. The doctors and nurses in the unit were caring and loving. On the other hand, the fellows and residents on rotation would stand at the end of my bed and discuss my case as if I weren't there. They never spoke to me but spoke about me. They talked over me, literally, as my body laid trapped in that bed. I was just a case study to them, not a person. I was never looked at in the eye. I was never acknowledged as a human being.

Their behavior baffled me and frustrated me. I never understood how they could be so callous. They knew I was coherent. My brain and my ears had not been injured in the crash. My hearing and cognitive ability were fully functioning. That made their conduct all the more maddening. I could hear them but because of the trach, I could not speak. If I could have, I'm sure my first words to them would not have been polite.

But these experiences all shaped me. I now consider myself an ardent patient advocate today. Did I know then that my career would be in healthcare and that I would rise through the ranks to become the CEO? No. But I knew God had a plan for me and I was ready to serve Him.

Once back on my feet, a neighbor, Charlie O'Toole, took me with him to work every day to get me out of the house and get my brain functioning again. I worked in the accounting office for him. I had been a business/finance major in college and it felt good to be an able-bodied, even with a slight limp, and intelligent contributor again. For the next six years, I stayed working for him. I will be forever grateful for Charlie's goodness and kindness.

What I learned then, and what has been the core of my daily life ever since, and continues to serve me in this evolving next chapter of my life, is that goodness and kindness have power beyond measure to affect another's life, and that gratitude has formidable power to affect our own life.

And these massive forces are always available and don't cost us a thing.

GUIDEPOST #1
KNOW YOUR ROLE

After a keynote address, any speaking or teaching I do, and in my mentoring relationships, I'm always thanked for my approach to what's most important in leadership. To make an impact, now and forevermore, there are five simple guideposts to follow.

Whether I'm talking with seasoned CEOs or young people just getting started in their careers or any level professional, the essence of my message is that to be a true leader in life, you have to take ownership of that role. Accept that YOU ARE a leader, no matter what title you hold. You are the leader of your life, regardless of career aspirations, and it's time to accept that truth.

I really don't buy into the term "born leader." The fact is that all jobs have a leadership role. You don't have to be born with a super gene. Or have a life-changing accident. The "secret sauce" is being willing to learn and grow. The most effective leaders continually monitor their role and contribution, AND they continually monitor their own level of learning, leadership, and service. That requires paying attention to your own behavior.

Of course it takes some level of "smarts" to be successful in business, and as you engage your brain, you need to remember being an effective leader does not require brawn. You can be a "tough" leader without being abrasive, belittling, or condescending (the three ABCs you want to avoid!). The captain of a ship is not bossy. He knows his role is to constantly monitor the instrument panel and the horizon to navigate the ship to its intended destination. When you are at the helm of a company or organization or non-profit, you may think you have to be forceful to drive your agenda. The opposite is true. Sure, you need to be strong and have a backbone, and yet you can be in command without being dominating or controlling. When you adhere to the guideposts presented in this book, you will see that shepherding the flock is easier because you are authoritative and you know your role.

The dictionary and thesaurus can give us many definitions and synonyms for the word leader. Among my favorites are captain, guide, and conductor. As a leader, especially a CEO, you need to understand the dynamics of the position, what is required of you and also what you do NOT need to do. This means you need to stay "above the fray." When I became a CEO in 1995, this was the most difficult concept to grasp. I felt that I needed to be engaged in all management matters and understand every nuance of information presented to me. I thought I had to do everything and be hands-on in everything. I was drowning in detail!

The chief issues like visioning and strategy were not being done—it was a day-to-day process. This was partly due to my age (42 years old in 1995) and my financial background (CFO prior to becoming CEO). Luckily I soon realized I had talented and capable people in senior leadership positions (and all levels of staff) and I could look to them to do their jobs. I didn't have to do it all. I was responsible for the whole and that didn't mean I had to have my hand on every piece. It was my job to make sure all the pieces were working properly and working together.

The CEO's job is to make sure that everyone involved in all those various pieces understand what they are working for, the end goal. As the conductor, you don't run from the violin to the cello to the trombone. You are not playing any instruments. You have selected the finest musicians to do their jobs. You are the leader up front making sure they all play the same piece together. Relinquishing control of each instrument and trusting your people to do their jobs allows them to do just that. They also all have to know what piece they are playing. People have to understand the vision and strategy or there's no buy in.

Your role is strategy and vision, being the guy or gal to take charge. My first major leadership stint began at West Jersey's Berlin hospital and the two years I spent there shaped my leadership skills for the future. Berlin was the smallest of West Jersey's four hospitals with merely 90 beds. Its size however enabled me to daily walk the floor and sit at nursing stations to discuss everything from employee relations to quality patient care.

I acquired all kinds of information about healthcare up close and personal, things like patient rounding, medical staff relations, community relations, employee reward and recognition, and so much more during my tenure there. My time at Berlin was short lived as I was asked to come back to corporate finance as CFO because the system was in a financial crisis. The CFO role paved my way into the CEO role and I was grateful, but I really missed my Berlin teammates tremendously. There was a unique bond there among nurses, doctors, environmental service workers, dietary, lab, security, etc. I saw how an organization could work together for a common goal. All the "instrument" sections were playing together in a harmonious symphony.

Back in finance in the middle of a crisis also allowed me invaluable insight into leadership. West Jersey was drowning. It was 1989, and we were running out of cash. My second in command came into my office and told me that we had $35,000 in cash with approximately $5 million owed to creditors. He also told me we were not going to make the next payroll and meet our debt service. Two things in business are paramount—you pay your employees and you pay your mortgage. Our CEO was out of the country and decisions had to be made.

We needed to borrow a substantial sum within a week as a bridge loan to get us over the hump. It was up to me to grab the conductor's baton. I called four banks and requested a meeting with them all. Three of them left the room telling me we were too much of a credit risk. One banker remained. And we got that loan. After we received the bridge loan, we never looked back. I vowed that we would never be in that position again. Twenty years later, Virtua has over $1 billion in cash and cash equivalents and is an AA-rated health system (by Moody's and S&P). Knowing your role means you have to step up to the plate, take risks and make big asks.

Leadership ability is always being honed. You have to constantly pay attention to what is going on around you, and you have to pay attention to your own behavior. When I took over as CEO, I had to learn to lead from a big stage. A helpful piece of advice was given to me by my former Chief of HR, Ed Dunn. When I took the reins at West Jersey, Ed said, "You're on stage every day and every eye is watching you."

No truer words were spoken. When you're the person leading, all eyes are on you, even when you don't realize it. Your authority is with you everywhere, not just in the board room. One day I was walking through the cafeteria at lunch time at one of our facilities, and I was lost in my thoughts. My head was down, my eyes to the ground, and I was not engaged with my surroundings. An employee approached me, concerned, and asked me if everything was ok. I was startled to realize that yes indeed I was being watched, even just casually strolling through the lunchroom. I assured the employee that everything was wonderful, and that I was just thinking about something. This was an eye-opening experience for me. From then on, I knew my role was to keep my head up, literally and figuratively. Truly, from that day on, I made eye contact and greeted those around me on every stroll through every hallway of every day.

As time went on, I matured in the position and gained wisdom, ascertaining how to lead from 30,000 feet and to stop sweating the small stuff. My role was to create a vision and global strategy and drive it through the organization. And that comes down to communication with people. As captain of the ship or the team, you don't want to be changing the game plan over and over.

The line of sight from vision to day-to-day operations at the ground level is critical. If the vision and strategies of an organization are complicated and change appreciably from year to year, employees will be lost. The job of CEO is to discuss the big picture everywhere and have all teammates understand why we are going in a certain direction. It goes beyond employees too and into the community and business community. You want everyone to have a clear picture of what your organization is about and does well.

To know your role means you are responsible for the big picture. Create vision, mission, values and strategies and inspire your stakeholders to believe in them. Then they will follow you. Thus, you need to keep the message simple but powerful. A simple vision and mission can take root and grow. Your role is to make sure that everyone knows their role. Managers can tell their employees that you doing your job of x, y, or z gives us the ability to meet the vision. The person answering customer service calls understands their piece in the big puzzle, as does the food staff, environmental services, the nursing staff, and on and on. Show employees their role in the vision.

For example, the billing department in a hospital is often a forgotten entity. I made sure every department at Virtua knew their importance. I told our billing department, "You broke records for cash collections! That money is going to patient care. That money is buying new equipment. Because of the hard work you do here, you save patient lives."

When a job is not just a job, but part of a bigger collective—saving patient lives—people care more about their work. They feel connected to the mission. They understand we're all patient caregivers. A great CEO can reach the hearts of their people and connect the line of sight of vision to their work.

We created 24/7 meal service for patients at Virtua. The dietary staff knew the joy they brought patients by providing tasty and healthy food all day. No matter what time a patient was admitted, they could get a good meal. The cooks took pride in their food. So much so that the local community would go to the hospital to eat and I still know that Wednesday is sushi day!

The housekeeping staff knew their significance. Certainly cleanliness is of utmost importance in a hospital, but these workers also had first-hand contact with patients. They were in patient rooms, interacting. Those interactions were a form of patient care. We held meetings at Virtua in the evenings allowing former patients to come back and give feedback on their care. One young woman recounted the story of how she was sobbing in her bed, distraught after losing her baby. The housekeeper had softly knocked on the door. "I hear you crying. May I give you a hug?" The patient said she will never forget that interaction. "She told me, 'Cry as long as you need. I am here for you.'"

You need to be able to connect the dots for all employees and departments as to the relevance and influence of their roles. At Virtua, it was my role to make sure everyone understood their role in patient care, and that everyone in the organization was valued as a caregiver. That was our focus and you need to stick to the core focus of your organization. As CEO of a healthcare organization, my focus was patient care and financial viability. You need to know yours.

Knowing your role means you don't get caught up in the latest buzz strategies or trends. Your role is to be strong and remain steadfast to keep steering the ship. There will be temptations to try the latest greatest scheme or strategy or tactic. Even if someone in California or Kokomo or Crazy Town did the hottest newest thing successfully doesn't mean you need to try it. There was a time when a buzz strategy in healthcare was to become an insurance company too and eliminate the middleman. It may sound like a terrific idea until the realization comes to you that this is outside the core strategy of a healthcare provider. I knew absolutely nothing about running an insurance company and I knew a lot about running a healthcare enterprise.

I had to make the decision, and communicate that decision and why we would not become the insurance company too. Your role as leader is to stay focused. Your job is to keep your eye on the prize and to keep the vision constantly in view and relevant to all. Everyone on board needs to know why the ship is being steered in the direction it is going. Humans have a fundamental need to know what is going on and why, so keep that information in circulation. Your role is to constantly remind people of their purpose. At the hospital system, it was my role to show each department how we are all Caregivers.

You need to understand that it is the CEO who grows the brand of the company. You are the face of the organization. You set the tone. A reputation of a company is associated with its leader, like it or not. No one truly enjoys the rubber chicken dinners at events, but part of your role is to be out there mingling. The role of the CEO is to be engaged, internally at the company and externally in the community. Part of your job is to get to know the people around the table in the community. When you or they need something, you know where to go, because you have established a connection.

I enjoyed getting involved in the community. I worked with our local Chamber of Commerce to host quarterly business seminars. I personally thrive in teaching and taking Q&A, and having a fireside chat format. You do what makes you most comfortable, but also be approachable. Show the community you care about the success of all as a whole. Share your knowledge. Those Chamber sessions were a win-win-win. The Chamber got the money, the attendees got terrific content, and Virtua solidified its reputation as a caring and giving company. You want your organization to have name recognition and you want it to be for good reasons. You can cultivate those reasons.

The CEO's role is strategic and inspirational and visionary. You are the one carrying the torch. The vision is the picture of the next five years. The CEO needs to remain in that space, the high vista. You can't take deep dives. If you go too deep, you end up hurting the organization. You have to tell yourself: That's not my job.

As a business leader, you have to know numbers, broad numbers. You might need a 3% operating margin to do a certain project next year, for example. As the boss in charge, if you are faced with a $4 million shortfall, you know either you're going to eat that four million or you find that four million. You have to understand numbers to make good calls, but your job is not just numbers. Your job is the grand scheme. You should only have three or four strategic goals in a year. You need to have goals that are doable, and you need to be able to communicate those goals.

Another aspect of knowing your role is to accept that no matter your position at the office, you are a leader at home as well. There were times that my workload came with a price—nights and weekends away from my family. In order to build a great company like Virtua, it required time and effort, and that meant a lot of time went into the job. When you take on a leadership position, you make a commitment to the role. That does not mean you throw in the towel on other vows in your life. You can maintain a home life and a professional life, but you have to know that it takes energy and focus. You can achieve work/life balance, but know that it is NOT 50/50.

Fortunately, I had a terrific wife. Mary Lee never blinked. She understood from the very beginning what leadership entailed. When we were first married in 1977, Mary Lee was the major wage earner in the family. She was a hair stylist working in two locations with two nights and a Saturday in her workweek. I was a staff accountant earning peanuts, working on my MBA. Our early years were a lot of hard work. A big Friday night for us was ordering a pizza and opening a bottle of cheap wine. Our first home was a townhouse. We couldn't afford the down payment on a house and interest rates were 11-12% at the time. As I started to earn more money, I assured her things were going to improve financially. Mary Lee was never concerned. She would tell me, "We'll get through it together," and we always have. From the day I met her and every day since, I proclaim my wife is a gift from God. By the time our two daughters, Kristen and Heather, came along, my financial situation had dramatically improved. Mary Lee was able to stay home with the children and we were able to buy a home in Marlton, NJ where we lived for 30+ years.

Perhaps not all spouses are so understanding, but they will be more so when you show your family that you care about them. In the same way you take care of your people at work, you take care of your people at home. You give them respect and let them know how much they matter. When you are home, be home. Give your attention. My children tell me that I was there for them during their growing up. I never missed their soccer games even if I got there at halftime. I went to parent/teacher conferences. When my phone rang during work hours, and one of my daughters or Mary Lee was calling, I answered—even if I had to step out of a board meeting to do so. That surprises people sometimes to hear that I took personal calls at work, yet why should I push my family aside simply because I have an important job? You can balance both.

Family is first. You will never regret it. When all the dust settles, when you have a bad day, when you are at the end of your career, they will be there for you. Certainly, it's not easy, for any party, but it's worth the effort. Even when you are exhausted, you can have a smile for your spouse and kids when you get home at night. All my vacations during my career were with my family. They were the priority, and even with my hectic schedule, they knew it.

The bottom line here is that being an effective leader is hard work but you can absolutely keep family first and work second knowing that there is no balance—the amount of time spent is not equal. You need to work hard at both relationships—the one with your career and the one with your family. I am living proof that it can be done. To know your role is to grasp that you have a leadership role at home and at work.

Another key to knowing your role is the boundary you must place on work friendships. The old adage of "there's no friends at the top" is interesting because it's true. Well, your leadership will be stronger if you make that statement true. If you are giving 100% to your organization and 100% to your family, there's not much time left to socialize with many friend relationships anyway. Mary Lee and I had some dear friends in our local community, but what I refer to here in this guidepost of Know Your Role are "work friends." You can maintain respect and connection with colleagues without outside-of-work friendships. I have witnessed many problems when leaders and subordinates built close relationships. As a CEO, it's imperative to keep some distance away from your team in order to lead appropriately. Being too close to teammates can cloud judgment and lead to poor decisions. And can give the wrong impression to those watching, and remember, you are being watched.

To be successful in your role and to keep boundaries does not mean to be totally detached. Taking a personal interest in the team is essential. You can do this without going to happy hour or dinner once a week. I have built cherished relationships with my senior leadership team. I care about them and their families very much. But friendships had to remain at a certain level.

There are many difficult decisions a senior leader must make. Some of them involve people. These decisions should not be made more difficult because of a "friend" relationship. A leader needs to be able to think independently and clearly without conflict. A leader should be able to go to his/her team and ask advice without the team thinking a decision will be clouded by a personal relationship. Thus, keep personal relationships out of the office. Be kind, caring and committed to your workforce, but keep a separation so you always know that you make decisions from an ethical non-biased place, and more importantly, that all who are watching you, at every level of the organization, have that same confidence.

To refer back to our conductor analogy, you respect all your musicians and treat them all with kindness and fairness. The person who gets first chair is because of their talent and hard work, not because of a special friendship. The entire symphony needs to see the conductor as an impartial leader.

No one said being the leader is easy. You need to keep your boundaries at all times while being gracious and paying attention to all. It's a lot of plates to spin. You must keep the vision and be able to articulate the vision so everyone knows what piece they are playing. You resist getting mired down.

You have to see the big picture and continually drive it forward. The only way to do so is to know your role.

GUIDEPOST #2
TAKE CARE OF YOUR PEOPLE

We were in the midst of a credit rating review. My CFO, myself, and members of our finance team had a three-hour meeting with Moody's to discuss our strategy and finances. Our financial results were outstanding and Virtua was going at an exponential rate. Virtua had been experiencing nearly fifteen years of solid success at that time.

The lead analyst for Moody's looked at me and asked point blank, "What's the magic bullet at Virtua?"

I explained to her that it was quite simple; it all starts with people and great people beget great culture. She nodded, but I could see that she wasn't totally in sync with my analysis.

Organizations that are built for the long haul have excellent employees and management in place. There really is no magic bullet—lasting success is the result of hard work coupled with care and compassion for your people. But how do you put that in a spreadsheet?

I came to Virtua in 1986 (then known as West Jersey Health System) as Chief Financial Officer, eventually becoming President and CEO in 1995. Over the years I have discovered that leadership is always—always, always, always—about how you treat people. The most salient aspect of leadership is to take care of your people. When you do, you attract top caliber workers.

Too many people believe that as they climb the corporate ladder, they have to change their focus. They wrongfully think that goodness and kindness are too soft for the boardroom or that gratitude is fine for Sunday morning, but during the workweek you have to put on a tougher veneer. That, my friends, is not the case. Realizing that people are the key to all achievement, prosperity, and success means you treat people right. All people, not just the ones who can do you favors.

You may have read other books or heard talks that mention people are your biggest asset, but have you taken it to heart? It does not matter if you don't consider yourself a "people person" or if your style of leading is more about profits and policy. Taking care of your people is what will carry you through the lean times and propel you to greener times. True leaders continually seek out how to be better, and to grow as a leader, you must extend yourself in new ways. That means taking a new approach to relationships with the people in your organization. The truth is that results—be it numbers, productivity, profitability, customer satisfaction, employee retention—don't fall from the sky. Results come from people. You take care of your people, and they will take care of you.

The basic tenet of this guidepost can be summed up in the phrase "love your neighbor as yourself." See your employees, all of them, at all levels, as human beings, as contributors to the overall end goal, and treat them as such. Call people by name. I had 10,000 employees and I knew many, many, many by name. Addressing someone by name reaps maximum reward. Even if you don't know someone's name (glance at their nametag!), look people in the eye, really see them, and give them your attention. This applies not only to your workforce but the cashier at the grocery store or the server at a restaurant. Never be too busy to affirm the presence of another.

Great organizations have great people, plain and simple, and you can foster the ability to surround yourself with such people. This means hiring, and firing, are equally powerful. You as a leader have to set the bar high. The organizations that do this well stay successful for the long term.

For me, the definition of "great people" are people that find joy in their work and are value-driven individuals. Obviously, that begs the question: Don't people also need to be competent in their particular skill set? Absolutely. There are many smart and skilled people to fill roles in organizations, but too many leaders simply begin and end the interview at skill set. In addition to skill set, you need to consider someone's "value set." These qualities of an employee are just as consequential. You can train ethical people to be better performers, but a "low values" person will destroy an organization over the long haul. When hiring or promoting, we must dig deeper into the individual's values, the things that drive behavior and decision-making ability.

The ability to "dig deeper" is critical when hiring a senior leadership team but truthfully applies to all staff. A diverse senior team in skills, thought, viewpoints and ideas is crucial. What can't be sacrificed are values. No matter what level of employee you are hiring, you need to look beyond intelligence into their character. The right people at all levels of the organization drive greatness because of traits such as compassion, kindness, humility, trust, integrity and caring. You can hire for both!

How to do so? As in most things in life and leadership, keep it straightforward and simple. For example, do panel interviewing for all new management hires.

Take four or five of your top talent management team-mates and let them interview a prospective manager candidate. These interviewers should be from different disciplines and do not require the same skill set as the candidate. The interview process here is not about know-how, but more about behaviors and attitude. The interviewers are trained to ask specific questions on how the candidate would handle certain difficult employee situations. After the interview, the panel discusses their thoughts about the candidate. If consensus cannot be reached on the candidate, the individual is not hired. You read that right. Do not hire. A bad management hire can set the organization back years. Make the right call from the beginning! You have to trust that among all those who are qualified are also many who are the right caliber of person. Being choosy is what takes your organization to the next level. A modicum of patience in the interview process pays off forevermore.

You also need to be able to fire people, and to train your people to be able to fire. When I was a young CEO at Virtua, I learned about the concept of "skeptics and cynics" from Tom Atchison, a healthcare consultant and speaker. Cynics are those folks lacking the characteristics I mentioned above. All organizations have them and know who they are, but typically do nothing to remove them. Severe damage can be done in an organization if you turn a blind eye and think that a person's skills outweigh their toxicity. Cynics dramatically affect the work environment around them and poison other employees wanting to do good work. It can take years to recover from the damage a cynic does to a department, a nursing floor or even senior leadership. Do not spend time trying to rehabilitate them. "Shake the dust from your sandals" and move on. When you keep only those employees with high standards, values, and morals, that is how you take care of your entire workforce. This effort pays off immediately and over the long term.

Skeptics, on the other hand, are healthy for an organization. They are capable workers and their values drive them to ask questions. Skeptics are not naysayers or looking to stir the pot. They are looking for reasons to believe. They need proof and will board the train once they are convinced of the direction and strategy. Eventually they will be your biggest supporters. Your senior leadership team should contain a skeptic or two. They inject healthy curiosity and can lead to new solutions. Welcome skeptics and weed out the cynics. And as they saying goes, be slow to hire but quick to fire. If you keep the bad apples, the good employees will go elsewhere.

Thus it is my belief that the Chief Human Resources officer is the most vital senior level position in the organization. The education, recruitment, orientation, talent review and all things people-related are under this person's influence. My Chief of HR during my time at Virtua was a terrific human being with top notch people instincts. An organization must have a strong leader in this role who can be open and honest with the CEO. If you do not have a strong HR leader, get one. The role is that important! Also, the recruitment team in your organization is an influential group in maintaining a stable workforce. This group should be highly qualified and expertly trained with the tools to release the cynics and hire and retain value-driven skilled people. Will you still hire some "duds"? Sure. Some people can seem like a superstar throughout the interview process, but their true colors show when they come on board. Your job is then to make sure your team knows to make the quick call regarding firing. Firing can be seen as harsh, but it's truly about taking care of people. Building the right team takes time and you get better at it as you go.

Another aspect of taking care of your people is to recognize and reward exemplary performers. As CEO, you must be engaged in the talent review process along with senior leadership. Twice a year, Virtua devoted two days to this Best People Review with all senior leaders participating, including me. We looked at all tiers of management to determine from where the next leaders in the organization were coming. We also determined which of our superstars were at risk of leaving the organization. Members of senior leadership, myself included would take these superstars to lunch, to discuss with them their futures and their value to the organization. These lunches were deeply appreciated by the individuals and served as a major retention tool. Spending time on your organization talent levels builds a solid succession plan for the future and is one of the most fundamental functions of senior leadership.

As the CEO, I found it extremely beneficial to welcome our new teammates to Virtua. Every week, I was at the orientation for new employees. The idea of taking care of people was not just lip service. Being greeted by the CEO makes an impression. I told a bit of my family history so they knew there was no silver spoon in my upbringing and how I personally wanted them to understand the importance of their role at Virtua. No matter what department, everyone was a patient caregiver. I realize not all CEOs take part in orientation, but in doing so it sets the tone from Day 1 that people matter to the organization. When people feel important, they are better workers. The presence of the CEO to welcome them on their first day was an obvious gesture to show we want all employees to get clear and consistent communication from the get-go. New staff were given my email address and encouraged to write me with ideas and issues. I did not interfere with the ability of my managers to manage but keeping an ear to the ground is imperative for any leader. Employees placed a high value on this connection. If your organization is too large, you can do this welcome address via video, but when you can do it live, do so. You will see the effect.

Reward and recognize your employees as much as possible. Virtua held a Superstar Awards night where we bussed 400 people to a fancy venue and gave awards for quality and safety, cost savings and community service. The annual event was always a wonderful night, and allowed us to shine a light on fantastic people. That spotlight of appreciation is not reserved for just one night.

We developed a program at Virtua entitled "The Virtua Experience." Stories of exceptional patient care and community service, along with the photos of the employees, were developed into high-quality professional posters that were displayed all throughout our facilities. From hallways to conference rooms to lobbies and waiting areas, staff and patients and visitors were able to witness the model of conduct that the Virtua team exemplified. Fellow employees enjoyed reading about their co-workers and seeing the recognition not just as an exhibit in the health system, but a true show of how Virtua cared about the people on the front lines.

Taking care of your people begins with people being seen and feeling their tangible worth in the organization. You have to bring in the human element. You want to develop a caring and kind culture, one so real and powerful that outsiders to notice it. We had people comment that "there must be something in the water there," because Virtua was such a different and refreshing place to be. This translates to any organization, not just healthcare. At Virtua, we wanted to be the hospital of choice. You may want to be the gas station of choice. The bakery of choice. The university of choice. The widget factory of choice. You can build that reputation.

From the front desk to the C suites, up and down the whole organization, when people are valued, it's palpable. Be people-centric. Customer-centric and employee-centric. There are volumes upon volumes and seminar upon seminar about customer service. Yes, of course, take care of customers. And take care of your internal customers, your people. Have regular employee appreciation events. At Virtua, we had cookouts at all the sites. Management teams served the food and thanked each person as they came through the line. We had summer festivals and holiday meals every year.

Recognize length of service with a free lunch or cake or even a hand-written card. People love to be recognized.

You can feel a great organization, the energy there. People are not walking by with their heads hanging low. Everyone carries themselves with a countenance of an upbeat optimism. Leadership allows a trickle-down effect of positivity, confidence and inspiration. You want an atmosphere where no one dreads coming in to work. How many times have you heard someone whisper, "What kind of mood is the boss in today?" Employees should NEVER say "My boss is in a bad mood." We all have problems, but we don't bring moods to the workplace. That is your job as leader, to keep an even keel.

When you do the right things for your people, they will respond in kind. The majority of the workforce is there to do good work. People do not get out of bed in the morning wanting to do a poor job. When you lead with the mindset of compassion, kindness and caring, that means just as much as the paycheck. Study after study has reported that being respected at work ranks as relevant as salary.

It was my commitment to make sure every department knew their worth to the organization as a whole. For example, the Customer Service Center needs to see how they fit in the puzzle as being caregivers. They are the first point of contact and service has to be second to none. Calls were taped and each month managers would select four calls of how customer services reps performed exemplary conduct. Each month I would select the Call of the Month and honor the incredible way our staff treated their callers. Sometimes our reps had to handle very touchy issues and we were blown away by the caring attitude of our employees. As CEO, I was there each month to say, "You guys are phenomenal" and to reward the Call of the Month with a gift card. Find ways to honor and recognize people regularly, not just at annual review time or the holidays.

Taking care of your people means creating a culture of honesty and ethics. As CEO, you have to practice it every day in every way. When you display back bone and inner strength, you empower others to do likewise. We instituted a corporate compliance hotline where people could voice their concerns. We received a complaint about our COO who wanted Accounting to write off a personal bill. I fired him. Yes, firing the COO is a big deal. Word got out that Rich lives by his ethics. One employee was fired for writing off false gas charges. Employees who are not ethical cannot be tolerated. This is for the good and welfare for all. People are comforted to know that the company they work for will do the right thing. Employees knew they would not get fired for a bad business decision, or simple mistakes, as those things can be corrected, but a person with no ethics will prove to be toxic and will infect the environment around them.

Creating a safe atmosphere where people's concerns are valid and there are no repercussions for speaking up shows employees that they are valued and their opinions are needed. We created "huddles" in which the nurses talked about their patients and their ideas every day. Everyone offered a "star" story from the day before. These huddles only lasted five or ten minutes but the impact was huge. Huddles were then held in every department from housekeeping to dietary to CEO staff. These short sessions were fabulous for idea sharing and building camaraderie and esprit des corps.

A company that is built on a people-first principle is an organization that allows their employees to learn, grow, and be successful in their roles, and as human beings. An effective CEO allows people to grow and to know they are supported. The reverberation is huge. Taking care of your people means you continue to discern how to understand them. The Myers-Briggs assessment opened my eyes early in my career. I hadn't understood people if they were not a "people person" like me. One senior leader, a smart guy, would never say a word in meetings. It drove me crazy. I wanted his input, but he would not speak up. After the meeting he would come to me in private and offer his knowledge. The Myers Briggs test helped me understand his personality and taught me how people differ. Then I knew to simply meet with him after our meetings to get his opinion. This kind of behavioral testing of senior leadership is powerful. You need your senior leadership to drive the philosophy and strategy, and you need to support how they do it if it differs from your style.

You are building an organization, and you are building people. In the end, nothing else really matters. We're all in this together. I realized fairly young in my career that my mission in life was to care for people. You may not feel that sentiment in the same way, but you must understand how crucial it is that the people in your organization, at all levels, feel valued. People want to be seen, heard, and understood. They may not always like your decisions or direction you take, but when they know their voice has been included and they know why the ship is being steered the way it is, they will come alongside. Perhaps not enthusiastically at first, but with the knowing that they are part of the chartered course.

As CEO, you are busy. But you are never too busy, or too important, to be nice. A polite hello, a smile, a nod cost you no time or energy or thought. These simple, practical tips can make all the difference to your employees. When you show respect, you are respected. When you show consideration, it is reciprocated. When you take care of your people, your people will do their best. That is how you lead to create a strong, continually improving, organization.

One of my favorite movies is the classic, *It's A Wonderful Life*. I look for new things every time I watch that film. It cannot be underestimated, or belittled, the impact we have on people every day, the amount of lives we touch. Do as George Bailey did and take yourself out of the equation for a moment. What would be the effect? Do you realize what's happening when you insert yourself back into the equation?

For me, taking care of people comes down to Love God + Love People = Success. That's it. Run your company and your life like that and you are successful. You'll live in the hearts and minds of people. Emulate George Bailey. It's not corny to be a great leader. It's your responsibility, and your lasting legacy.

GUIDEPOST #3
TRUST YOURSELF

I was featured in a book by Tim Malloy and Billy Martin on sales leadership called *ONE THING: Insight from top executives on what it takes to be a great leader.* The One Thing they culled from me was to factor in gut instincts when making key decisions. Call it what you will—gut instinct, intuition, a strong knowing—this information is just as viable as the facts and figures on the page. You don't make decisions from your head alone. You enlist all your capabilities and that includes using your intuition.

Yes, review the data and also engage your ability to sift through the "hard" evidence and you also apply the unseen advantage of experience, wisdom, and the "sixth sense." The more you use it, the better you become at trusting the inner knowing.

To develop your core muscles in your abdomen, you know to exercise. Sit ups, crunches, planks. To develop your gut instinct, you also need to exercise it regularly. In order to better access your intuition, make a daily practice of taking some quiet time. Unplug from the world and let your mind be still. Sit in silence. Enjoy the quiet. Breathe deeply and slowly. Doing this daily allows your busy brain to take a pause and allows the voice of intuition to be heard.

When you are faced with a decision, make a comparative list with your gut instinct possibilities and the data driven information. Reach out to colleagues who have no data on the matter and no influence and no repercussions from the decision. Simply provide enough information and ask for their gut feeling on the matter. Include their responses on your comparative list. You will see how intuition can be a powerful player. Also be sure to use trusted advisors who will be honest with you in the event you are unable to release personal biases or emotions that are distorting your evaluation of the situation.

The best way to get to know how well you use your intuition is to pay attention. Monitor how often you feel your gut instinct pointing a certain direction. Notice if you acted on it or not, and what the results were. Keep a journal of these occasions. The more you notice how well you do using your intuition and the beneficial outcomes, the more you will be able to trust yourself to make decisions using gut instinct. Albert Einstein called our intuition a sacred gift. Use it.

When discussing great leadership, history is rife with examples of this intangible power of gut instinct. As a CEO, I was faced with many difficult decisions related to people, strategy, finances and politics, just to name a few. Certainly some financial decisions are straightforward and you need to follow the numbers—but some are not so easy. In 2008, Virtua began construction of a new $700 million replacement hospital in Voorhees, New Jersey. We had been planning this project for years, since 2002. The first $100 million was our cash investment in the project. We would recoup these dollars when joining the bond market in 2009. So what happened? The stock market crashed and we could not sell our paper. I had $100+ millions of steel erected on the site with few choices other than continue to fund the project with Virtua's cash or abandon the project.

One Monday morning, in early 2009, during one of our strategic planning sessions with my senior leaders, I was asked, "Rich, how do you want to proceed? What should we do?"

This was a perfectly legitimate question to ask the CEO. We had hit the decision point. I told my team that I would answer the question in the next couple of days. I met with some members of the medical staff who urged me to move forward. However, if we could not get to the bond market in 2009, it would significantly damage our cash reserves and place our other services in jeopardy. The easy way out was to end the project and maintain our current aging Voorhees location. But I knew this new hospital, if built, would be a game changer for patient care in our community—not only for our residents but for our clinical staff as well. Our community and staff had spent years modeling the new hospital and the excitement was palpable. The final decision was mine and it was time to tell my team and my Board of Trustees what we were going to do.

I felt in my gut that I had to build this hospital and things would work out financially. It was time to move. I gathered my team together, told them we would slow the project down a bit but we were moving forward with the build. I received total support from my team and it was onward!

In May of 2009, my CFO informed me that there was a window to sell our bonds and he was heading to New York City to do so. I happened to be in Washington DC at the time for some meetings on Capitol Hill. I asked him to let me know the progress of the sale. That afternoon, my cell phone rang and when I saw his name pop up on my phone, my hands started to sweat.

He told me that not only did we sell the issue, but we oversold the bond issue which lowered the cost of the capital. The tide had turned and things were looking up! The first part of the sale goes to retail investors who were buying the paper so fast that the large institutional investors were concerned that the issue would be largely gone before they could jump into the fray. The truth was that given Virtua's financial strength as a health system over the years, investors were looking for a safer investment and were leery of the stock market. To say I was relieved was an understatement!

From the roof of the old Voorhees hospital the day of our move.

The new Voorhees hospital opened in May 2011 and is the jewel of the South Jersey community. Our community and our clinicians viewed it as the most technologically advanced hospital of its kind and with Virtua's great caregivers added to the mix, it was a "grand slam."

As I look back on this gut decision, it was easy to see that the numbers and risks associated with the project

From the roof of the new Voorhees hospital.

could have made me shy away from making the choice I did. However, what I knew to be true was that trying to maintain the existing old, crumbling structure was not the right way to go. Trusting my inner guidance (and faith, a guidepost we will get to later) allowed me to get through the decision process and a successful conclusion was reached. I also now see how those words are also a metaphor. Too often we try to maintain an old existing "structure" or habit that is crumbling or at least no longer serves us. To create something new, although a risk, is much better for all in the long run.

Mastering trust in yourself can take time. You have to pay attention to all the times you listened to your gut and it turned out well, and vice versa. When did you go against what your inner wisdom was telling you and you regretted it? Part of building the trust muscle is paying attention and also listening. Listening is a key skill and it possibly could be its own guidepost, it's that meaningful. You have to listen to your gut and that takes practice. You also have to listen to others, really listen. The more you listen, the more you learn. The more you learn, the more you are able to trust your instincts, in all decisions.

When in doubt, listen more and talk less. Life is not a podium. Being a CEO is not about being the mouthpiece. You must become a good listener. This is the path to trusting yourself. You listen to your own wisdom, and you listen to that of others. Never interrupt when someone is speaking to you. Make eye contact and listen intently. Be present all the time. If you are a good listener, people will know they can approach you. They will trust you to listen. You will thus trust yourself at a deeper level.

As CEO, you are the coach. Skillful coaches have the expertise to listen intently to their client and provide a summary back to the client making sure they have attained all the relevant information. Then they ask more questions. Coaches never need to solve issue for the clients—the clients eventually do it on their own. It's the same with employees—they will get to the answer, you just guide them there. Do not jump in and be the problem solver. Listen carefully to their concerns and ask more questions and eventually they are solving their own issues. Listening also builds a bridge between you and others. People feel seen and heard. When you ask people what they think, inclusion of their opinion brings buy in. Give people credit publicly for their feedback and ideas. Trusting yourself is knowing that you do not have to be one with all the answers. This takes a lot of pressure off your shoulders.

We implemented Employee Advisory Groups at Virtua. Each group consisted of about twenty people and they would bring issues to the forefront, from speed bumps in the parking lot to patient care issues. These groups gave employees a voice, and also the ability to solve problems. When one employee, Nancy, suggested speed bumps due to an increased speeding problem on campus, I said, "Do it. Figure it out. Talk to maintenance. Get some numbers and report back next month." She did. You do not have to be the one to know how do we do it; let the group figure it out. They will. This group got the project done, and Nancy and the group got the credit. The Employee Advisory Groups became the hot group to join. We assigned a senior leader to every issue and included people in the solutions. And much got done.

You trust your intuition more the more you use it. If you are in healthcare, you may be aware that doctors have their own culture and sometimes do not collaborate well. They're experts and their priority is patients. As CEO, you have to learn how to work with their culture. It's a matter of trust. The doctors needs to trust the CEO. The CEO needs to be able work with them, and still be strong and have big shoulders. The bottom line, always, is relationships. You need to meet with them in person and face any issues head on with honesty and directness. You can be tough but fair. You stand by your values and principles, doing the right thing, and always communicating. At Virtua, I met with the doctors frequently and each year we held an annual "State of the Hospital" dinner at a beautiful venue. During the cocktail hour, I made a point to chat with everyone before delivering the message.

I also put together a leadership program for doctors, which was decidedly not well received at first. This four-day retreat meant physicians would be away from their patients and was a tough sell at first. I gathered a mixed group of ten doctors and opened the retreat on a Thursday. To say their eyes threw daggers at me would not be exaggerating. I came back on Monday to close out the program. Over the weekend, the docs had gone through leadership training and had social time together. There was a total difference in the air when I was there on Monday. I was embraced, literally, and was told how the program had changed their lives. We went on to do ten more groups after that and it became a desired objective to be selected for the retreat. We had the best leadership program in the country. I trusted myself, my gut, that it was the right thing to do, and we established deeper trust among all.

Trusting and listening affects your relationship with all people, at work and at home. I listened to my wife, my daughters, and I listened to my employees. I asked people what they thought. I valued the opinions of others. No matter how heated an exchange may have gotten, I never spoke over others. Well, okay, I'm human, sometimes it did happen. The point is to get all the information on the table and proceed with wisdom. That is how you matriculate in trusting yourself.

As you are going up the ranks, it can be beneficial to have a life coach, someone you can talk to intimately and confidentially. We all need that level-headed someone who comes from a different perspective, someone that we trust, someone that we can discuss anything with—a person detached from the work site. There will be big decisions to make as a leader and we all need someone with whom to bounce our ideas. It could be a spouse, significant other, close friend, or a paid coach. I was fortunate because my wife Mary Lee was an excellent coach for me.

Part of learning to trust yourself is to have confidence in your ability to make things happen, even if you do not know how just yet. Your job is to be able to see the big picture and know what needs to shift to achieve the end game plan. The execution of the strategy does not have to be known immediately. You simply know what you need to accomplish. The how is not always known up front. As a seasoned leader, this gets easier. As a newbie, you may have to be more conservative in your plans, but one thing is steadfast—you have to have courage. Courage comes in the doing.

Experienced leaders can give a 5-year plan every year and I advise new CEOs to build a 3-year plan. You have vision with a strategy. As a new CEO, you are building relationships and you are building your confidence—confidence in yourself and the confidence that others have in you. Sometimes young leaders try to fake it until they make it. I say don't do that. Know what you're talking about. You're not going to be able to fool people. If the team views you as weak or not having answers or strategy, they will not have confidence in you. Trust can take time and it comes in incremental bites.

Experience is our greatest teacher and the only way to amass experience is to put yourself on the line. You have to trust yourself to speak and act according to your values and intuition. The only way to build that muscle is to use it. Your role is to the get team on board. Your role is to relentlessly drive the vision. Your role is to make the tough calls regarding strategy. I've seen a CEO tell the CFO "cut what you need to cut." That is not a strategy. Slash and burn only works for a couple years to meet the bottom line, but the organization and employee/customer satisfaction declines. Cutting people should be the last resort. I made sure our senior team had photos of employees right in front of them during budget review sessions. I wanted them to understand that these are people that count on their wages to support their families. Employees are not faceless numbers. This simple measure put a different light on budget review.

Alongside with trusting yourself is honoring what I call the "fire in the belly." All the best leaders I have met over the years have this trait, which is tantamount to telling people exactly what is on your mind and being passionate about it. As CEO, you have convictions and need to stand up for them. You have to be able to stand firm. You garner trust and respect when you are firm in your beliefs.

I became a CEO in 1995. Shortly thereafter, in 1997 we decided a merger was in order between my health system (West Jersey Health System) and Memorial Hospital of Burlington County. This would consolidate health services in two neighboring counties, improve quality, and reduce duplication. We completed the merger (forming Virtua), but I was not seeing the quality and safety and financial results that the community deserved.

In early 2000, I gathered the entire management team in our conference center. My tone was stern and direct, telling them our results were basically "average"—50th percentile—and that was not good enough. We needed to be top decile in all of our results—our community deserved that! I told them that we (all of us) were going to be accountable to results and if that was not what they wanted to do, Virtua would assist them in exiting the organization. I felt the fire in my belly and I took action. You have to remember too that employees are jaded. They have been through the ringer. It can be hard to trust when they have been through too much crap. You've got to walk your talk and prove yourself. Over and over and over. You can show them passion. You can show that a person can get upset for the right reasons and handle the situation with dignity and respect. You have to show that you are going to do what it takes to get the job done. You harness the emotion for the right reasons and people see what is important.

Fire in the belly can be tough-minded, accountable and sometimes a bit angry. It also contains kindness, caring and a deep concern for people's welfare and a consistent approach to leading change. You can still be a "nice" person and not be a pushover. Honoring and trusting my gut instinct and the fire in my belly have always led me to the proper action and profitable results. Harnessing these "soft" skills can make you very forceful as a leader.

GUIDEPOST #4
HONOR YOUR VALUES, VISION, VULNERABILITY

When I made the decision to go forward with the building of the new hospital, it was the perfect trifecta of honoring my values, my vision, and being vulnerable. What if things went haywire? It was my neck on the line. But I knew it was the right thing to do. I had the vision for this new community facility which was a beacon for the values I held dear and the values we promoted at Virtua. And this project was a complete win for all. We were able to build the hospital right on budget and the construction was a godsend to the community that had been feeling the effects of the economy nosedive. We worked with union leaders and construction companies and subcontractors. So many people were put to work because of this project.

Incorporating our vision and values all throughout the process, when it came time for the actual move to the new hospital, we had the brightest engineering minds—students at MIT—lay it out. Moving operations from one hospital to a new one is tricky endeavor. From patients and premie babies, to staff and visitors, to supplies and equipment, organizing a safe and efficient move was paramount. The move plan was a triumph and has now subsequently been used by other healthcare systems.

My values and vision include letting bright people have the opportunity to do their thing. When designing the new hospital, we had those using it—doctors, nurses, and patients—give their input which was turned over to the engineers. Who best knew where to put the supply rooms or how to lay out the patient rooms than those who would be working there daily? Giving ownership to the employees in this way created a vested interest in the overall vision and the finished product. Something that may seem like a minor detail, like a stool at every bed for face-to-face conversations, showed our integrity and that being caregivers was the #1 priority.

A big part of vision, values, and vulnerability is culture. That word culture gets thrown around a lot and can mean different things to different people. For me, culture is how you function every day as people working together.

What I discovered as CEO of Virtua is that we had one over-arching culture, and yet each hospital had its own sub-culture. And that's okay! The key is that all know the lead purpose and what needs to be done to move forward. I realized that we needed to implement a certain strategy for any particular goal and everyone on the whole team knew it but could get there in different ways, based on what they did in each hospital. One size doesn't fit all, and does not have to. Cultures can be different and still operate effectively for the overall game plan.

As the CEO, you talk to each group about strategy and vision. You give the line of sight for each team to get to the end goal and give them the freedom to choose how they will do so. You cannot shove your ideas down people's throats. You cannot be heavy handed and "lay down the law." Such a tactic will backfire. That is why you work on trusting yourself so you have the confidence to do what is right, even when it's not easy. Culture is a lifelong job; it shifts and changes as new people come in and you have to go with the flow, all the while keeping everyone focused on the big picture. Let nuances happen at the local level. Give specific timelines. And let them do it their way.

Being a part of a merger was the eye opener for me. West Jersey was a big system and Memorial was merging into it and did not want their culture over-ridden. We formed a board that governed 50/50. We had to come up with a new name (Virtua was the winner) and we had to build name recognition around it. Memorial kept their name and became Virtua Memorial Hospital. Change is hard and you have to accept that it takes time. The job of the CEO is to be relentless in keeping the vision and values intact. And also to be accessible. I had to deal with the chaos and the emotion. I was open to suggestions and people came to see that I cared. Everyone is vulnerable. Honor that. I knew that patient care suffers when the culture is not good so the leader must keep his/her finger on the pulse of the culture at all times. You set the direction and let them come along in their way. You maintain the global culture and let each location operate their culture as long as they follow the values, strategy and vision. You have hired good people and good people do good things.

Vulnerability is worth it, for all involved. When I first became CEO, corporate headquarters and one hospital were in Camden, New Jersey, one of the poorest cities in the country. The row homes near the hospital were owned by slumlords and many of our employees lived in those houses. My Board chair, Bill Bowman, and I approached a rehab organization with the express notion that our people needed to be home-owners. We worked together with the city and local politicians to acquire these homes, rehab them, and have the bank secure their mortgages. This program was called RENEW and was met with surprise and skepticism at first.

One employee, Juanita, rented one of the slum houses and there was no trust in the city of Camden. She approached me one morning and asked, "Are you stealing my house from me?" I replied, "If you can trust me, I am going to make sure YOU OWN IT."

She had been an angry non-trusting person because she was left disappointed too many times, but she changed. Her attitude shifted when she realized that the values of the organization were not just lip service. Juanita's was the first home rehabbed. She was so proud when it was completed and she held a big open house. Two blocks, twenty houses. Virtua invested in not just the homes, but the people. Employees were beside themselves with pride. Those homes are still beautiful today. Juanita and all the others felt rewarded for their hard work. They had never experienced people delivering on their promises. People do not have to make a million dollars to feel special. They need to be valued.

Years later we had to make the tough decision to close the in-patient services at the Camden hospital. It was an emotional decision for me, and I had to make sure that we turned the facility into something beneficial for the community. I swore that I would never shutter the building and abandon it. We needed a strategy for this big building to be workable even if it no longer was for inpatient services. It became a resounding success. We leased it, giving a fair price to tenants, and also a slight profit to us. We kept the ER and added primary care doctors, behavioral care and a dental facility. A detox unit took over some space. A charter school came in. Rutgers University opened an incubator for startup businesses. The bottom floor was rented to the Camden Police Department so it was a secure place. The hospital became a community asset and a model of hospital transition to another community facility. Even with the closing of a hospital, we still drove our visions and values for the community as a whole. In order to make this happen, I had to go before the community leaders and church leaders to present my plan, before going to city council. The pastors supported the vision, and this beacon of light in an underserved community was formed, and is still there. The Camden building offered needed services and the level of care was second to none.

This was an example that the vision of the organization needs to support the community, and the CEO needs to be able to explain that vision properly. It goes back to knowing your role. The CEO is front and center, and creates and sells the idea. Others implement it, but the CEO has to get the acceptance. People need to be able to look you in the eye and know that you stand firm. Even if there is backlash, in fact, especially if there is backlash, you must do the right thing. You must be the one to honor the vision and values of the organization. They don't care about your words, what you say you have to deliver.

Sometimes you step out of the box and make some unpopular decisions as CEO, but in the end, everything circles back to taking care of your people, your employees and the community. In Camden, there was no supermarket. People had to go out of the city to get veggies or healthy food. Part of Virtua's vision and values was community service. We had a mobile food fan brought in to underserved areas and it would always sell out. We had farmers bring in fruits and vegetables, and had dieticians explain nutrition. We provided health and wellness education, and did diabetes screenings, blood pressure checks, and chronic disease education. Virtua worked with a local charity, the Joseph Lacroce Foundation, that provided a van for mobile dentistry. If dental health is not taken care it can foster other disease.

The Philadelphia 76ers partnered with Virtua for nutrition and exercise education. Basketball clinics were put on every year and every kid got a new pair of sneakers. Scott O'Neil, president of the Sixers, also showed up every year with me and our employees to work on a selected location in town to fix up. Renovate. Paint. Garden. We did it to show our appreciation for being part of the community. The 76ers' new state-of-the-art practice facility was built in Camden. I became active in the Boys & Girls Club, volunteering and coaching, and speaking to the kids about careers. Most kids that age worship athletes or musicians. I brought in doctors and nurses so they could have new professions to aspire to. Employee engagement and community engagement. When it is sincere, everyone can feel it.

We continued to create ways to be of service to the community. And to our employees. When we had to close the in-patient services at the Camden hospital, folks rightfully wondered about their jobs. I told employees myself that a plan was in place to be able to move them to the other hospitals. Jobs were held for them. To this day, I am thanked by staff in nursing, dietary, security, etc., for keeping them employed.

Do not dismiss the little things. Like in a marriage, what you do on a daily basis shows what is important to you. Attitude is synonymous with values and vision.

When I entered the building every morning, my head was up and I had a smile on my face. I greeted my security guard, Fred, on the first floor. I rode up the elevator with employees to the fourth floor, and everywhere I went from then on, I greeted my teammates with a "good morning" and "have a great day." Everyone in the building was my teammate.

How you carry yourself is contagious. If you want to create a caring culture, it starts at the top. If I do not behave the way I wish others to do, how do I expect my team to do it? You must lead by example and you will see the ripple effect, and it can start as simply as everyone starts to smile and greet each other. That is all part and parcel of driving your vision. Consistency is crucial. I regularly walked around and talked to people. I engaged them personally, asking about family, their weekend, or anything fun they were doing in their lives. People love interacting with their senior leaders in this way, but the real issue is showing that you genuinely care about your teammates. People will spot a phony, so be sincere, in all ways. That means you are vulnerable. Truthfully, as humans, we all are, but we sometimes think we can build walls around ourselves. You do not want to be on guard. You as leader want to show others that being genuine is what counts.

Do not be afraid of being vulnerable. When you screw up, admit it! Set the example. There have been times I did not act the way I wanted. One instance that comes to mind involved two of my leaders who made a decision that I did not like. I was upset. Angry. I yelled at them. That was not like me. The next morning I called them in to my office, and they were rightfully panicked about what was going to happen, but I apologized. I explained, "I'm not teaching you anything good by acting like that." They had been shocked by my outburst and then shocked (but truly appreciated) my personal apology. Everybody makes mistakes. Your job is to be the teacher, the guide. By being vulnerable and admitting when you are wrong, you are showing what it is to be accountable for your actions. You are always leading by example, so your behavior matters. Later in a meeting one of the two who I had yelled at shared the story with one hundred managers, stating "I learned that day how to be a better leader. Rich admitted he was wrong. And it's okay to do that as a leader. I'll take that with me my entire career."

Too many leaders think they need to wear an impersonal facade all the time. What your people really need from you is to be real. Talk to them. Involve them. Include them. Keep driving the vision. When Virtua's customer loyalty scores were not optimal, I discussed with my Nursing director team and told them how much I appreciated their hard work and dedication. If I berated them over poor scores or admonished them, then they would feel dejected and more poor scores would follow. If you lead in a positive, supportive way, your team will follow your example.

If your vision is to be customer service driven and results oriented, you are the engine. In healthcare, our focus was to be caregivers. Caregivers need to be taken of as well. I would often pull up a chair at nursing stations to simply ask, "How are things?" The more you visit with your teammates, the more they will be comfortable and see you as a concerned leader, a regular human, not just the CEO or boss. They will be able to relax and engage in real dialogue. My employees weren't afraid to tell me anything. They knew that they, or their manager, would not get in trouble for a candid conversation with me. They knew I had time for them. I'd also sit in the cafeteria at lunch, available, approachable and accessible to any employee.

Shared governance was important at Virtua. Patient care issues were addressed by the nurses and they needed to know that their concerns were not being ignored. I would pop into their discussions. One time in the Neonatal Intensive Care unit, the nurses were wanting milk warmers.

I simply asked, "How many machines do you need?"

The answer was forty-two.

"How much do they cost?"

$1,000 each, was the reply.

"So, $42,000," I stated. "Don't you think we could get a donor to cover that cost? We're buying them." They were stunned. I reminded them to not be afraid to ask. You have to make the ask is a lesson we learn over and over in life.

When working with my managers, I would coach them to focus on WHY they made the decisions they did. When you keep asking the question why, you are able to drill down to the core of the issue.

We would review the week with "What went well? What could be better?" I spent a lot of the time in the field as working directly with employees gave me great joy and cemented our values. Our nurse managers were empowered to talk with me about what was going on in the units, be it technology, patient issues, staff issues, anything. One example was the time and attendance system in place was a pain. It took the nurses away from patient care, so we fixed that system. It took time, but we fixed it. When your employees know they have your ear and you have their back, you can work together to make their job easier, and in healthcare, their job is caring for patients.

Some of my leaders later told me that the management meeting in early 2000, where I expressed the fire in my belly that average was not good enough, was Virtua's turning point to excellence. Right after that meeting, I instituted Virtua's five-point STAR initiative. The patient was at the center of the STAR, with the five points being Best People; Quality/Safety; Patient Satisfaction; Resource Stewardship; and Caring Culture. These points of the STAR have evolved over the years but conceptually it's the same as it was all those years ago. Every employee at Virtua understands the STAR culture. It's everywhere, it's simple and recognizable. Some of the managers in the room that day thought this was going to be a "flavor of the month" program, but it has survived and flourished.

Soon after implementing the STAR initiative, I contacted GE (our Enterprise Partner) and asked them for help in instituting a tool kit. In early 2001, we incorporated Lean & Six Sigma methodologies into Virtua and reaped over $40 million in bottom-line savings over the years. I continued to seek out GE for other tools they used in measuring people and measuring products and services. GE has been a valued partner of Virtua since 2001 and truly assisted us in becoming an accountable organization. By 2003, all managers were held accountable to their STAR dashboards and their annual goals and objectives. I was intolerant of managers who placed unmeasurable items in their goals and objective package. Everything had to have a measurement attached to it. Your job as CEO is to maintain consistency so people know what to expect. You have to stick to the game plan. Keep measurements the same for years so people know what to strive for. Employee cannot do constant change. Do not change your metrics all the time. You can carry the passion and the vision by keeping it consistent.

Virtua achieved top decile hospital in three of the four measurable STAR components, Quality & Safety, Resource Stewardship & Employee Engagement, and top quartile in Customer Satisfaction. Virtua became a national player in training. We were only $1.3 billion in revenue, but were much "bigger" because of our knowledge base. Our people went around the country speaking and training other healthcare organizations. The STAR Initiative was the defining culture for Virtua and vision, strategy and values emanated from it. This was the line of sight for the organization. Yet in the beginning, this was a risk. Again, I had to take the chance that this type of training would be beneficial and profitable. I invested a million dollars to train my people. Not all healthcare companies would do so, but it was a risk that paid off handsomely.

We ranked every person in every department by top performer, valued contributor, or needs improvement. If someone ranked Needs Improvement, I asked their manager, "Are they a value-driven individual? If so, give them a different position. Put them in a job they can do well." Some then moved to Top Performer. If a person was ranked NI and was not a value-driven individual, they had to go. This forced ranking system lasted six years and then we didn't have any more people who received Needs Improvement. We were able to move on from that evaluation system. That way of looking at employees took us from average to an outstanding organization. We became top 5% in the country in employee engagement, and we never had a shortage of nurses or any staff. We were the place where people wanted to work.

A leader's values and ethical behavior are never negotiable. You should lead your organization with one thing in mind: Do the right thing—all the time. My team at Virtua knew never to cross the line or get close to it. Frankly, I would not allow unethical behavior to exist on my senior leadership team. Never tolerate a lack of integrity from anyone. Make sure everyone in the organization understands that it is immediate grounds for dismissal if this type of behavior occurs. Trust begins with the values and ethics of the top person in an organization. As I now retire, people tell me they remember me most for the "person" I am; not the CEO I was. This is a very important distinction.

Being genuine may seem like a vulnerability, but it is a strength. And honestly, is there any other way to be? Be the same person at work as you are at home. Bring your values with you everywhere you go. Your consistency as a value-driven individual will be the biggest asset you possess.

One of the values that I held for myself and for my people was to be a lifelong learner. I worked in the South Jersey community for 40+ years and we were blessed with many engaged and caring leaders. My colleagues on South Jersey Chamber Board and the Select Greater Philadelphia Board were terrific people who built remarkable companies. Two outstanding companies were Wawa and GE, and I soaked up quite a bit about leadership by listening to Chris Gheysens of Wawa and Jeff Immelt of GE. Jeff, a very hands-on leader, was instrumental in providing his knowledge of being a results-oriented organization. I've already mentioned how the GE toolkit of Six Sigma, Lean, Session C and more took Virtua to the next level. I knew healthcare needed tools to reduce variation in process because healthcare is probably more laden with wasted processes than any other industry. Jeff provided two of his master blackbelts to meet with our executive team and the rest is history. Virtua became one of GE's first enterprise accounts using manufacturing tools to improve patient outcomes and lower costs.

Wawa, a convenience store and gas station chain, has a large presence in the greater Delaware Valley and the East Coast with over 800 locations. Wawa is known for their exceptional customer service (and their hoagies). I was on a panel with Chris one morning and I asked him why Wawa doesn't have automatic sliding doors at the entry point to the store like many supermarkets and convenience stores. He said it was because when people entered into a Wawa, they would hold the door open for an exiting customer or another entering customer and greet each other with a "Thank you" or "Have a good day" and a smile. This simple interaction creates human connection that not would have happened if the doors opened automatically. Everything they do at Wawa is geared toward a positive customer experience. Absolutely brilliant!

The common denominator for both these leaders is that they care about their people and built impressive teams underneath them. The traits of successful leaders are the same whether you are the CEO of a small company of 50 people or the CEO of GE or Wawa. I learned many valuable lessons from the leaders around me and became a better CEO because of it. Pay attention and listen to others, there is always a lot to that will benefit you. And don't be afraid to make the ask. Virtua would not have gleaned all that incredible training if I had not asked for a meeting with Jeff.

This value of learning was evident in how Virtua treated employees. Virtua paid for staff degrees. One manager in the housekeeping department, Carol, wanted a degree. I told her, "Go get it. We'll pay for it." She got her Bachelor's degree and then wanted to become a Six Sigma master blackbelt. She did. And she went on to get her Master's degree too. The ability to grow at Virtua was limitless. I often took middle managers to lunch and would ask: What do you want to do? What is your dream?

These lunch meetings made a big impact and getting a call for "lunch with Rich" was a major acknowledgement of their potential. One nurse manager was especially gifted and bright. During a lunch meeting, we discussed her running a women's program for the whole system. Many employees went on to achieve many things in their careers, and they were grateful for how they developed as people.

The responsibility lies with the CEO to carry the vision and values of the organization. The only way to accomplish this is to acknowledge that doing so requires your vulnerability. Take the risk. You won't regret it.

GUIDEPOST #5
KEEP FAITH

The George Bailey effect is real, and it's immeasurable. I didn't realize until after I retired the impact I had had on people. People will to this day come up to me and thank me. They thank me for doing what I have laid out for you here. By operating my life and leadership with these guideposts, I have unwittingly inspired those around me. I went in for my flu shot this year, and the nurse had tears in her eyes as she thanked me for my service. "You always put us first," she told me. I do believe my biggest accomplishment was the people I could help, professionally and personally. To make a difference in someone's life at work means that you have affected their whole life.

We may not all be able to see ourselves through the eyes of the people we work with every day, but what if you could? What would you see? Do you like it? Do you want to change it?

My accident at age twenty-one set me on a path that would allow me to show my gratitude for being alive and for being able to be an influence on people and a great organization. I knew it was my mission to take care of people. Your mission may be something different; maybe you want to create the best widget on Earth. So be it. Whatever you are doing, you are a leader. You hope to leave behind a legacy, even if by osmosis, of giving and caring. Hence, the last piece of advice to give you is to keep faith. That means to keep faith in yourself and to keep faith in something larger outside yourself. My faith is an integral factor in my leadership ability. My faith is in God. Whenever I needed to know what to do or when to do it, I prayed.

Knowing the right thing to do, and then doing it, requires faith and trust. I got burned sometimes, we all do, but I continued to trust. If someone took advantage of my trusting nature, that could be painful certainly, but it was temporary. I never stopped trusting. It always mattered to me that people could feel my trust. If that trust was betrayed, that was ultimately on them. I will never say that I trusted too much. Always trust, always keep your faith in yourself and in your fellow man. It hurts sometimes but many more blessings come of it.

As you progress in your career, you will see that there are not a lot of risk takers out there, so it's even more important to have the CEO be the one who can do that and be that. You drive the strategy and values so employees don't have to take the risk then. How can you do that day after day? With faith.

There are differing ways of practicing faith among each of us, but the truth is, when we are in a difficult situation and it comes down to doing the right thing, faith shows us what that is. Faith allows you to take that right action, even if it's not easy.

That's another fact to accept—being the leader is not easy. Life, and leadership, are hard. Being a CEO or head of a department or any position where expectations of you run high is not for the faint of heart. You need to expect lows. Know that you will face challenges and struggles. Understand that you will have tough days. Realize you will be misunderstood and disagreed with and not liked. When you can expect lows they will not able to knock you off your game. Weathering storms is part of the job. You are up for the task. There are difficult challenges. I once had to fire my COO. That was a hard time for me. I was down in the dumps and didn't want to go to work. That is when my coach/mentor/wife, Mary Lee, said pointedly, "Get your head out of your ass and go be a CEO." That direct kick in my butt re-energized me and reminded me to get back in the game. My people needed me to lead. And things at work got better than ever.

Expect lows and seek out joy.

Being a leader means there are no days off, and there are no "off" days. You have to keep your chin up and keep going. There are no "bad" days for a good leader. When I get up in the morning, I put my feet on the floor and I thank God for another day, another opportunity to improve on the day before. For me, real joy comes from my relationship with the people around me and my relationship with God. Going to work every day should not be drudgery. We should wake up with a sense of purpose and joy. That requires faith. Is it all sunshine and rainbows? Of course not. There were areas of my day that were not uplifting, especially dealing with politics. However, I put these less uplifting sequences in their proper perspective—how were they helping my 10,000 teammates at Virtua?

Joy is in the eye of the beholder, and if you seek, you shall find. For many years of my tenure at Virtua, we gave a performance-related bonus to our employees. If Virtua did well, our employees should reap the rewards of that performance. I got the greatest joy every year writing that letter to our team, thanking them for their hard work. It lifted my soul to read the emails from my employees telling me how much these bonuses meant to them. They bought Christmas gifts for the kids, helped pay the mortgage, helped with the care of another loved one, and on and on. This is real joy.

Another thing we did at Virtua was create a fund, called the Cares Fund, after the financial crash of 2008. People were struggling. Spouses had lost jobs, mortgages could not be paid, it was a nightmare for many. So we initiated this fund with contributions from people across Virtua to support those in need. The kindness and caring of the Virtua team was astounding. Those in need were helped and deeply appreciative. We also had a catastrophic funding mechanism housed in the Virtua Foundation (the fundraising arm of Virtua). If someone had a house fire, the death of a child, or some other event, a major gift was provided by our Foundation to the family to help them through such hard times. There is no more rewarding joy than helping others. And we can do that every day.

Leaders have the ability to lead a joyous organization. As I look back over the last two decades of my career, my moments of fun and joy were often the "small stuff." A teammate stopping me in the hallway to tell me they are a first time grandparent or coaching a group of elementary school kids from Camden in a basketball game against the Camden County Police department or spending a day at the Boys and Girls Club talking to the kids about their future. Revel in the small stuff, reflect on success with your teammates and simply have fun.

FUN is necessary. Spend time with employees in fun. Know how to work hard, and know how to play. You can't be killing your employees every day. Take employees to lunch, bring food in, recognize acts of caring. Honor people. The more you do so, the more joy you will cultivate and the less on-the-job lows you will experience. You can tip the scales with a bit of effort towards fun. And that goes for at home too. During my drive home, I would reflect on the day and what I could have done better. I would also pull out the positives. I would end with my commute with gratitude and a vow to bring my best self to work the next day. I also would bring my best self in the front door when I walked into my family. Never go home and say, "It was a rotten day." Look at your family and home life as support and respite, a soft place to land. See your kids laughing and playing and feel that energy. Join in the fun. My daughters regaled me with stories of their day. I was the Saturday morning breakfast chef. Those times together can refuel you.

Leaders much refresh themselves. Looking at past accomplishments is another way of doing this. During my quarterly Virtua leadership meetings, I asked our team (500 managers in the room) to reflect on great leadership moments—moments of people helping people. The stories were wonderful! Often they would bring tears to our collective eyes. These moments reflect the culture and values of the organization. This sharing was uplifting to the entire team. Taking a pause to see the good work being done is fuel to the soul to keep going, and allows others to keep the faith.

Simple joys bolster us. Feeling good about our work, our colleagues, and our organization is invaluable to the bottom line. And as we all know, real joy does not come from attaining money. The accomplishments, the realization of one's aptitudes and talents, the teamwork, the recognition, these are true joy. Success does not equal money. Success is about a life well lived. Life is all about people, always. We all play a role in each other's lives.

Recently I sat in my car outside my daughter's house, right after I left from babysitting my grandkids and contemplated at how my life has evolved. The joy I feel now in these relationships—with my beloved wife, my cherished daughters, their husbands, and my grandchildren—is a gift that I am grateful for every single day. I have relationships with former employees, colleagues, and members of the community that have stood the test of the time. I know it is because I have applied these guideposts all throughout my life and career.

Taking care of people is always the right thing to do. I have enjoyed the ride, and I keep faith. I keep faith in God, in my family, in my ability to serve others no matter what role or title I carry, and I keep faith in humanity. When we do the right thing, when we lead with our values, we are able to lead successfully, and we are able to create a legacy that leaves people in a better place.

Having faith in others can buoy you. Faith, like trust, is reciprocal. When you show your faith in your staff, it is returned. All these elements work together. I loved listening to my nursing staff. They were the heartbeat of the hospital. Theirs is a life and death job. We put relaxation rooms with lounge chairs on nursing floors so they could destress on breaks, take it down a notch and come back refreshed. It may be common sense to know that nurses (and other occupations) work hard, but to be in the trenches for a day can give you new appreciation. I worked a 12-hour shift with one of our nurses, Anne. I wanted to know the issues. (Our corporate lawyer was not happy. "Don't touch any patients!" I was warned.) I helped Anne with everything. Admit and Discharge paperwork to patient care. The patients didn't know I was the CEO of the hospital. They thought I was just shadowing. I got the full experience and we hustled for those twelve hours. When it came time to report out to the next shift, we had been on our feet all day, grabbing a bite to eat when possible and showing extreme dedication to patients. Was it exhausting? Yes. Exhilarating? Yes.

Another day I spent in the kitchen at one of our hospitals. James the cook showed me how to cook chili. We cooked, we cleaned, we served, we did dishes. Not only does this in-the-trenches time broaden your horizons, it builds rapport, which builds faith and trust. And creates joy. I did housekeeping one day. Cleaning the rooms on the floor for a day made me so proud of our staff. Changing sheets. Disinfectant. Caring for people. I rode with our paramedics one night, seeing the crazy situations they face daily. They made me wear a bulletproof vest as part of their territory included some rough areas. We went to a drug house and a shooting scene. These EMTs are the front end of care, a special breed of medical personnel, and I have the deepest respect.

To walk in the shoes of another, to know what they do, is a game changer. Appreciation abounds both ways. When you can form a bond with your departments, you are establishing faith in each other. You show that you are there for them. Post-retirement, that's what people remember—that I was there for them. And I remember that my most fulfilling times were not spent in my office.

I personally believe all good stems from God. If we as individuals are doing good things, God is a part of our lives. To be a leader in today's environment, it's important to know that you can ask for God's help every day. I know there are times that we feel lost and are searching for answers. Sometimes we wonder if God is listening—is He there? He is there—trust me! There were times as a CEO that I struggled with some major people issues at the senior level. All I could do was pray. I realized that God may assist me with signs but it is up to me to act on it.

Every morning on my way to work, I prayed for the full thirty-minute commute. As a Catholic, I pray my rosary. I ask God for blessings and help in everything. God never gets tired of listening—even to small requests. Ask Him anything. Prayer is essential because it gives us strength and renews our soul. It is my belief that we simply cannot reach the pinnacle of success without God's help. True success is maintaining joy in one's life. I believe Jesus was the world's greatest leader because of His great love. He also provided us with a guide to true leadership. So why not ask Him to guide us through prayer. God is at the root of all joy, success and happiness. He wants us to do well in our careers and He also wants us to take care of each other. When we pass on to the next life, we will not be asked how financially well off we were, but how we made the lives of those around us better.

To focus on faith and joy, you need quiet time in your day. Even if you do not pray, time for quiet reflection is essential. There is so much noise in our world today, we need a break from it. You need time to think and vision. When driving to work, turn off the radio. Don't have music or news or books on tape. Just be with your thoughts. Think of what you are grateful for. Think about how you can grow and how you can grow your organization. During the day, take fifteen minutes away from meetings and people. Close the door and close your eyes. Breathe deeply. Reflect. Ask for clarity and guidance. This fifteen minutes a day is building a better person and a better leader. It's critical and not being done enough today. Put your phone down. Get off social media and spend time on yourself.

When you take this quiet time, you return to a calmer perspective. You are able to see the forest and the trees. You will see solutions. You will be able to connect the dots for others. See everything that happens as a learning, as a gift. Stop looking for the grand prize out there and realize that the grand prize is the little things and the big things, like family and what brings you joy. The more you able to take care of yourself, the more stamina you will have for the job.

Not every day will be a banner day as a leader. There will be moments when things seem to be going all wrong. These are the times you need to dig deep and keep faith. You need to review these guideposts and implement them. Take a walk among your employees and help them with their issues. Keep a warm smile on your face even during trying times. People will appreciate the positive response you show every day and will reciprocate. Take care of your people. Know your role. Trust yourself. Honor your vision, values, and vulnerability. And always, always, always, keep faith.

WRAPPING IT UP

As a leader, you keep on keeping on. You must care about your organization until your very last day. Don't check out. The job is not about prestige or money. It's about what you were able to create, and leave behind. The world will keep turning, technology will keep evolving, and innovation will keep creating new ways of doing things, yet the guideposts presented here are evergreen. They work for any organization in any industry for all time.

You can create a career and legacy to be proud of. The making of a great CEO requires tools, yes, but you have to also breed what's on the inside, the passion and the caring of people. If you have that, then you layer in dedication, discipline, and drive. Remember that there are no short cuts. Nothing is handed to you. You have to show up, day in and day out, and do the work.

I was blessed with great nurse directors who loved their employees and patients. I too had a real affection, admiration, and respect for our nurses and doctors. Walking the patient floors was deeply meaningful and informative for me. The time I spent with them discussing patient care issues was the highlight of my day.

Every day I would stop at our nursing stations to talk our nursing heroes. They are daily witness to life and death, so many highs and lows with their job. I think about them often, as I do of nurse Joanne.

The physicians I worked with were incredible individuals, and intensely loyal to their patients. If anything got in the way of caring for patients, like a hospital policy or procedure, I would hear about it! And it wasn't always a pleasant conversation.

I have so many wonderful physician stories, and only a few I'll share here in these pages. These folks epitomize the high caliber, high caring staff we had at Virtua. Dr. Ron Librizzi, a perinatologist, is one of the most brilliant minds I've encountered in medicine. He's also able to combine his extensive knowledge and expertise with a caring bedside manner. Ron always makes time for people. When my daughter called me in a panic during her first pregnancy because the baby's heartrate was elevated, I immediately called Dr. Librizzi. He asked if she by chance was using cocoa butter on her belly to reduce the potential for stretch marks. She was. Ron explained that he had done a study that showed the use of cocoa butter led to caffeine entering the blood stream and thus affected the baby's heartrate. My daughter stopped using the cocoa butter and the baby's heartrate returned to normal.

Dr. Nermin Lazarus, a primary care physician, was the perfect person to take on a new endeavor for Virtua—a practice built around the health and wellness of women exclusively. Nowadays, this is common, but back then my idea of a women-centric primary care practice was a bit radical. Dr. Lazarus has a caring approach, is a great listener, and spends a significant amount of time with each patient. When we were building our women's health product line, I asked Dr. Lazarus to go on a Philadelphia talk show to talk about women's health. She was excited to go on TV and was a smash hit!

Time and time again, our physicians embodied all that is good in healthcare. My own family physician, Dr. Sam Weiner, is a crowning example of the values I hold dear. When I sit with him for my annual physical, he listens intently as he sits right across from me, face to face, eye to eye. He gives me his full attention and is focused on my needs and questions. Sam also understands that I know more about myself than anybody else and he shows me that respect. The best physicians make the patient a partner in the care process. Leaders do that as well. You make your teammates partners in the process of growing an organization that all can be proud of and grow with, personally and professionally. That is the hallmark of true leadership.

Everything one does as a leader should be for the benefit of others. Before I began a negotiation, I listed all the key stakeholders that would be affected. I determined the positive and negative effects on the stakeholders and then decided whether to move forward or not. Remember, keep your focus on people, people, people. Every decision may affect someone.

I am faith-driven, you may not be, but these guideposts will serve you well. As the workforce, and society, continue to change, the heart of the matter is still the same. If you do these things and work hard, you will have the fortitude to take the risks needed. Don't be afraid to move forward. Take advantage of opportunities when they come.

Know that being a leader is about evolving as a person, and we can do that until we die. Thank you for reading.

EPILOGUE

A horrific auto accident in April of 1974 nearly took my life, but in fact it gave me my life. That defining event forged me into who I would become, and how I would navigate the path of life choices, personally and professionally.

As I looked out at the sea of faces in the Knott Arena on Graduation Day 2017, I was awash in pride. I felt the calming presence of God and gratitude for a life lived by my values.

I delivered the commencement address, giving a snapshot of my story and a quick synopsis of my leadership tips. With a grateful heart, I closed by thanking them, students and administration alike, for allowing me to be a part of the Class of 2017 as I had not been able to walk my own graduation processional forty-three years earlier.

The entire arena arose in a standing ovation as tears streamed down my face. Here was the kid from South

Philly who had accomplished a lot in his career, and yet never felt prouder. I saw Mary Lee in the front row, my strong, loving best friend and mentor over the past forty years, and our eyes met. She smiled and nodded and applauded.

My mind's eye flashed back to the early days of Mary Lee and me when she was a hair stylist at my uncle's beauty salon. I used to visit the shop from time to time to say hello. Mary Lee was a beautiful young woman—tall, long dark hair, and a wonderful personality. I wanted to ask her out on a date but given that I was in a leg brace at the time and quite self-conscious, I delayed any kind of invitation. Finally, one day I mustered up the courage and asked her out. The rest is history! I proposed to Mary Lee in the shrine of the Grotto of Lourdes at Mt. Saint Mary's where the Blessed Mother overlooks the college from the mountain. As I sit here writing this forty years later, my love for Mary Lee has grown immeasurably.

As I embrace this next chapter of my life, that of retired CEO, I look forward to speaking and mentoring and sharing my insights with leaders and organizations about true leadership. With faith in yourself, and a greater faith—whatever that may be for you—real greatness and contribution can be achieved.

Life is bigger than dollars. Your genuine and lasting worth is the good you do and the legacy you leave behind. When your efforts live on in the hearts and minds of the people you have touched, then you are able to look back on your career with deep satisfaction.

How do you want to impact lives? We all affect others, every day, and we don't realize our influence in every interaction. Imagine your own retirement. When you look back on your career as a leader, do you want to be remembered as a beast or a blessing?

If you were to do a life-in-the-rearview-mirror review, I would guess you would want to see scenes of a life well-lived where you were able to assist in the development of others and build a strong organization, and maintain sound connection with your family. I enjoyed the movie, *The Gladiator,* with Russell Crowe, and I suggest you watch it from a leadership perspective. Maximus had the respect of his soldiers because he cared for them. They didn't just respect him, they loved him. He'd won their hearts and minds. His demeanor and his motto was that of strength and courage. Maximus also had the same respect from his fellow gladiators. His mental courage and moral fiber is what real leadership is. Being able to inspire exhausted people in tough times is pure leadership. That is the task we are faced with today.

People didn't always like or agree with my decisions, but they did understand my decision-making process and why I did my strategy. You don't get everyone's love but you need their respect. Truthfully, you don't want everyone to love you; that means you are not doing your job.

It's my wish that my words here have helped you in some way. I consider this a book written from the soul and I trust this basic simple approach to leadership may enhance your life, in ways large and small.

Please reach out to me and share your story. Connect with me at www.richmillerleadership.com. It is my wish that as I take my last breath, I am still giving, still supporting people.

Let me close with my favorite line from *The Gladiator:* "What you do on earth will echo in eternity."

Thank you for devoting your time to these pages. Now go and devote yourself to being the leader you know you can be, in your career and in your life. That is how you create a lasting legacy.

ACKNOWLEDGEMENTS

First and foremost, I would like to thank Jesus and His Mother Mary for loving me and giving me the ability to lead a great life and great organization.

Secondly, I want to thank the love of my life and inspiration in life, my wife, Mary Lee. Without her constant support, none of this is possible. Also, my two beautiful daughters, Kristen and Heather, made life rewarding, fulfilling and wonderful.

Thirdly, thank you to all the beautiful people who crossed my life during my forty-year career, and special thanks to Maria Simonetti, my assistant for ten years.

Finally, thank you to Kelly Epperson Simmons, my ghostwriter, who put together my ideas and words so beautifully. Thanks, Kelly!

ABOUT THE AUTHOR

Since 1998, Richard P. Miller has served as president and CEO of Virtua, a non-profit healthcare system offering a full continuum of primary, preventative, wellness, acute, and long-term care.

Miller led Virtua in innovative directions by creating a values-based culture defined by the "Star Initiative," adopting Six Sigma, and transforming a group of community-based hospitals into technologically advanced regional medical centers. In addition to an enterprise alliance with GE Healthcare, Virtua formed clinical alliances with nationally renowned organizations such as Penn Medicine and The Children's Hospital of Philadelphia (CHOP).

Rich Miller has been nationally recognized with appointments to the Leadership Advisory Council of the Joint Commission Center for Transforming Healthcare (CTH) and to the Governing Council of Healthcare Executives for the American Hospital Association. He is a Fellow of the American College of Healthcare Executives and served as a trustee of the National Quality Forum.

Miller serves on the Operating Committee of the Board of Select Greater Philadelphia. He served on the Board of Trustees of the University of the Sciences of Philadelphia, was Chairman of the Board of Trustees of the New Jersey Hospital Association, served on the Governor's Committee on Benchmarking for Quality and Efficiency, and the NJ Healthcare Access Study Commission. Miller has served on the boards for the American Heart Association, March of Dimes of Southern New Jersey, and is a past chairman of the Chamber of Commerce Southern New Jersey Board.

Among his recognitions, Miller was honored with the New Jersey Hospital Association's 2017 Distinguished Service Award. He received the inaugural Lifetime Achievement Award by the Chamber of Commerce Southern New Jersey. He was named Human Resources CEO of the Year by the HR Department of the Year Awards. Miller received the CEO IT Achievement Award from Modern Healthcare magazine, was named Healthcare CEO of the Year by the Philadelphia

Business Journal, Lean Six Sigma National CEO of the Year, Distinguished Citizen of the Year by the Boy Scouts of America, and received the New Jersey Business Hall of Fame Lifetime Achievement Award from the New Jersey Junior Achievement.

Goodwill honored Miller with the Helms Award for spreading goodwill through leadership and philanthropic involvement. Miller has been named among the 100 Most Powerful People in New Jersey Business by NJBIZ magazine, one of the 50 Most Powerful People in Healthcare by NJBIZ, a "Person to Watch" by *Philadelphia Magazine*, and recognized nationally on the list of "291 Hospital and Health System Leaders to Know" by Becker's *Hospital Review*.

A graduate of Mount St. Mary's College, Miller earned his MBA from Southern Illinois University. Miller received an honorary Ph.D. from Mount St. Mary's University in Humane Letters (for Leadership) in 2017.

For more information or to hire Rich to speak, contact Rich@RichMillerLeadership.com.

9 781649 707215